St. Patrick's Day

Jennifer Blizin Gillis

Heinemann Library
Chicago, Illinois

SOUTH HUNTINGTON
PUBLIC LIBRARY
HUNTINGTON STATION, NY 11746

J 394.268
Gillis

© 2003 Heinemann Library
a division of Reed Elsevier Inc.
Chicago, Illinois

Customer Service   888–454–2279
Visit our website at www.heinemannlibrary.com

All rights reserved. No part of this publication may be reproduced or transmitted in any form or by any means, electronic or mechanical, including photocopying, recording, taping, or any information storage and retrieval system, without permission in writing from the publisher.

Page layout by Ginkgo Creative, Inc.
Printed and bound in the United States by Lake Book Manufacturing, Inc.

07 06 05 04 03
10 9 8 7 6 5 4 3 2 1

Library of Congress Cataloging-in-Publication Data
Gillis, Jennifer Blizin, 1950-
  St. Patrick's Day / Jennifer Blizin Gillis.
      v. cm. — (Holiday histories)
Includes bibliographical references and index.
Contents: It's St. Patrick's Day! — St. Patrick's Day from town to town — Honoring St. Patrick — Early Life — A new religion — St. Patrick's Day in the Colonies — The Irish in America — Gifts from Ireland — An American idea — The Wearing of the green — Shamrocks — Harps, Shillelaghs, and little people — Irish tradition, American holiday — Important dates — Glossary — More books to read — Index.
  ISBN 1-4034-3504-9(HC), 1-4034-3689-4 (pbk.)
1. Saint Patrick's Day—Juvenile literature. [1. Saint Patrick's Day.
2. Holidays.] I. Title: Saint Patrick's Day. II. Title. III. Series.
  GT4995.P3G55 2003
  394.261—dc21

                              2003007829

Acknowledgments
The author and publishers are grateful to the following for permission to reproduce copyright material:

Cover photograph by Bill Greenblatt/Getty Images

p. 4 David Binder/Stock Boston Inc.; p. 5 Robert A. Davis/AP Wide World Photo; p. 6 Stephen J. Carrera/AP Wide World Photo; p. 7T Derek Pruitt/AP Wide World Photo; p. 7B Martin Jacobs/FoodPix; p. 8 Bettmann/Corbis; p. 9 Corbis; pp. 11, 15, 16, 20 Hulton Archive/Getty Images; p. 12 Stapleton Collection/Corbis; pp. 13, 27R Richard Cummins/Corbis; p. 14 The Granger Collection, NY; p. 17 Heinemann Library; p. 18 Peter Lennihan/AP Wide World Photo; p. 19L Bettmann/Corbis; p. 19R Reuters NewMedia Inc./Corbis; p. 21 Museum of the City of New York/Corbis; p. 22 Joseph Sohm/ChromoSohm Inc./Corbis; p. 23 Stone/Getty Images; p. 24 PhotoDisc; p. 25 Matt & Kathleen Brown/Taxi/Getty Images; p. 26 Hulton-Deutsch Collection/Corbis; p. 27L Sandy Felsenthal/Corbis; p. 28 Morton Beebe/Corbis; p. 29 Kevin Fleming/Corbis

Photo research by Kathy Creech

Every effort has been made to contact copyright holders of any material reproduced in this book.
Any omissions will be rectified in subsequent printings if notice is given to the publisher.

Some words are shown in bold, **like this.** You can find out what they mean by looking in the glossary.

30652001408717

Contents

It's St. Patrick's Day!

Store windows are decorated with paper shamrocks. There are cardboard cutouts of leprechauns. People are wearing green clothes, green hats, even green paint on their faces.

*The man on the left is dressed like a leprechaun (LEP-ruh-con),
a kind of make-believe Irish fairy. The girl in the middle of
the picture is wearing a shamrock on her pin.*

It seems as though everyone is Irish on
St. Patrick's Day. In fact, there are more
people of Irish **descent** in the United
States today than there are in Ireland!
Everyone is happy for this chance to
honor Irish-Americans.

St. Patrick's Day from Town to Town

Across our country, many towns celebrate St. Patrick's Day. In Chicago, Illinois and Savannah, Georgia, workers pour green dye into the rivers. Other towns have big parades.

Maybe you will eat some green food today. You may have a St. Patrick's Day party or treat in school. But why do we do these things on March 17?

Honoring St. Patrick

People celebrate St. Patrick's Day to honor St. Patrick. Patrick is the **patron saint** of Ireland. He lived in Ireland hundreds of years ago. He died on March 17, 461.

This picture shows Saint Patrick telling the snakes to leave Ireland.

There are no snakes in Ireland. Some people believe that is because St. Patrick sent them all out. That story may not be true. But Saint Patrick did change the way the Irish people felt about **religion.**

Early Life

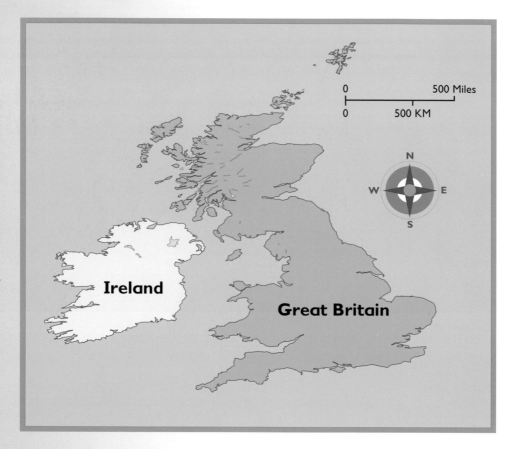

Patrick was born in what is now Great Britain. His parents were wealthy people who owned a lot of land. But while he was still a boy, Patrick was taken. He was sent to Ireland to work as a **slave.**

Shepherds are people who take care of sheep. Long ago, they used to stay in the fields with the sheep day and night.

For many years, Patrick had to work as a shepherd. But one day, he escaped. He went home to Great Britain and became a **priest.** After a few years, he decided to go back to Ireland.

★

A New Religion

In Patrick's time, the people of Ireland were called **Celts.** They were fierce fighters. They stole things from other countries. They took people to be **slaves.** They even killed people as part of their **religion.**

Patrick went from village to village. He
taught the Celts a new religion called
Christianity. This new religion said that
it was wrong to kill people or take slaves.
Soon, most of Ireland was Christian.

★

13

St. Patrick's Day
In the Colonies

In the 1700s, Irish people began to come to America from Ireland. They came for freedom of **religion.** The thirteen American **colonies** welcomed people from Ireland and other countries.

This painting shows General George Washington with some of his soldiers during the Revolutionary War.

The first American St. Patrick's Day celebration was held in Boston, Massachusetts in 1737. Later, the colonies fought the **Revolutionary War** against Great Britain. During that war, General George Washington used "St. Patrick" as a secret password on St. Patrick's Day in 1776.

The Irish in America

During the 1800s, there was not enough food in Ireland. Many Irish people left to find work and food in the United States. Many of these people moved to Boston and New York. They were happy to be in a new country, but they missed their homes in Ireland.

Life was difficult for Irish people. Their jobs were hard. Many people treated them cruelly. Celebrating St. Patrick's Day was a way Irish people could show that they were proud of being Irish.

One hundred years ago, some businesses hung this sign in their windows.

Gifts from Ireland

The Irish brought many things to their new country. Much of our folk music comes from Ireland. These children are step-dancing, a style of dance that came from Ireland.

There have been many famous Irish-Americans. John F. Kennedy was the 35th President of the United States. Sandra Day O'Connor is a judge in the **Supreme Court.**

Sandra Day O'Connor

John F. Kennedy

An American Idea

St. Patrick's Day parades were an American idea. After the **Revolutionary War,** a group of Irish **veterans** started a club. It was called "the Friendly Sons of St. Patrick." People in this club began to march every year on March 17.

At first, men and women just marched in the street. Then, they began to make the parades more exciting. Soon, bands marched and played music. In 1875, the first float was used in a St. Patrick's Day parade.

This old picture shows a float—a large stage that carries people in a parade. Long ago, floats were wagons that were pulled by horses.

The Wearing of the Green

These men are carrying an Irish flag.

For many years, people have worn green on St. Patrick's Day. That is because Green is the **national** color of Ireland. The Irish flag is orange, white, and green.

Ireland is an island that gets a lot of rain. Rain makes green grass and green moss grow. So green clothes are a symbol of the green fields of Ireland.

Shamrocks for St. Patrick's Day

A shamrock is a small, green plant with three leaves. Some people believe that St. Patrick used the shamrock to explain the Christian **religion** to the **Celts.** Each leaf stood for a part of the Christian religion.

On St. Patrick's Day, many people decorate
with cutout shamrocks. Shamrocks grow
wild all over Ireland. Today, shamrocks are
a symbol of love for Ireland.

Harps, Little People, and Shillelaghs

A harp is a symbol of St. Patrick's Day. Harp music has been played in Ireland since St. Patrick's time. Old **Celtic** art often shows people playing harps.

This drawing shows a Celtic man holding an Irish harp.

Leprechauns and shillelaghs are
St. Patrick's Day symbols, too. The Irish
believed that Leprechauns were fairies
called "Little people." The little people were
full of mischief and tricks. A shillelagh was a
kind of weapon that the Celts used in fights.
Today, important people in parades carry a
wooden walking stick. They do this to
remind people of shillelaghs.

★
27

An American Holiday

Americans have come from different countries around the world, including Ireland. Celebrations, symbols, and foods from these other countries have become a part of American life.

28

Americans honor St. Patrick on March 17. And on that day, we say "thank you" to the Irish people. We celebrate the special gifts they have given to our way of life. We are proud that the United States is one country, made of so many different people.

Important Dates

St. Patrick's Day

March 17, 461 (or 464)	Death of St. Patrick
March 17, 1737	First St. Pat's celebration in Boston
March 17, 1762	Groups of Irish immigrants walk through the streets of New York to celebrate St. Patrick's Day
March 17, 1776	George Washington uses "St. Patrick" as secret password during the **Revolutionary War**
March 17, 1812	Friendly Sons of St. Patrick formed
March 17, 1824	First St. Patrick's Day Parade in Savannah, GA
March 17, 1875	First St. Patrick's Day float appears in a parade

Glossary

Celts people who lived long ago in Ireland, Great Britain,
and parts of France

Christian religion that follows the teachings of Jesus Christ

colony group of people who live in a new land

descent came from

national having to do with a whole nation

patron saint person who is thought to be especially good
and who is very important to a country or group of people

priest man who gives his life to God

religion what a person believes about God

Revolutionary War war that the thirteen American
colonies fought to become free from Great Britain

slave person who must work for someone else for no money

Supreme Court most important court of law in the U.S.

veteran person who has fought in a war

More Books to Read

Berendes, Mary. *St. Patrick's Day Shamrocks.* Chanhassen,
MN:Child's World, Inc, 1999

Rosinsky, Natalie M. *St. Patrick's Day.* Minneapolis, MN:
Compass Point Books, 2002

Schuh, Mari C. *St. Patrick's Day.* Mankato, MN: Capstone
Press Inc, 2002

Index